A Quiet Confession Manual

SHEILA HILLIER

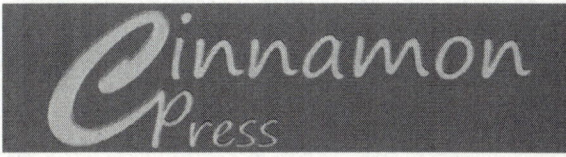

Published by Cinnamon Press
Meirion House
Glan yr afon
Tanygrisiau
Blaenau Ffestiniog
Gwynedd, LL41 3SU
wwwcinnamonpresscom

The right of Sheila Hillier to be identified as author of this work has been asserted by her in accordance with the Copyright, Designs and Patent Act, 1988 Copyright © 2010 Sheila Hillier
ISBN: 978-1-907090-12-7
British Library Cataloguing in Publication Data A CIP record for this book can be obtained from the British Library
All rights reserved No part of this publication may be reproduced, stored in a retrieval system, or transmitted in any form or by any means, electronic, mechanical, photocopying, recording or otherwise without the prior written permission of the publishers This book may not be lent, hired out, resold or otherwise disposed of by way of trade in any form of binding or cover other than that in which it is published, without the prior consent of the publishers

Designed and typeset in Palatino by Cinnamon Press Cover design, Mike Fortune-Wood, from original artwork 'St Michael' by Carlos Paz used by kind permission of Alpacaware
Printed in Poland
Cinnamon Press is represented in the UK by Inpress Ltd wwwinpressbookscouk and in Wales by the Welsh Books Council wwwcllcorguk

Sheila Hillier is a medical sociologist who has researched in many countries, especially China. She is now Fellow and Professor Emeritus at Barts and The London, Queen Mary's School of Medicine and Visiting Professor at the School of Public Health and Primary Care, Chinese University of Hong Kong. She and her husband live in London and in France, near Avignon.

Acknowledgements

Versions of some of these poems first appeared in *Agenda Online, Ambit, Orbis, Guardian on-line, Brittle Star* and *The Interpreter's House*.

'Pollux and Castor, elephants' was a runner-up in the National Poetry Competition, 2006.

'A Sleeping Spell' was a runner-up in The *Mslexia* competition, 2006.

'Jack Lattin of Morristown' won the *Poetry News* Hamish Canham Prize in 2009

Margaret Kelleher's book *The Feminisation of Famine* provided details for 'The Practice of Running', Rebecca Sprang's *And They Ate the Zoo*, alerted me to gastronomic exoticism in 'Pollux and Castor, elephants' as did Regina Harrison's work to the religious software of the Hispanic Empire, which informs the title poem.

I acknowledge my huge debt to Todd Swift, who has been my tutor over the past several years.

Contents

I

Internal Exile	11
Pollux and Castor, elephants	12
Hackney Blue Hour	14
Bedroom Ware	15
Dreaming of the Dead	16
Border Crossing	17
Public Art	18
Lucia's sky-blue cupboard	19
Because We Are, I Think	20
She revisits the Embankment	21
Violet, Doris, Hilda, Joyce	22
Retribution	23
Buddleia Detectives	24
London Light	25
To die is different from what anyone supposed	26
Morning Duties by Sunlight	27
Emperor of the Kitchen Garden	28
Insulting Peacocks	29
Menus for a Requisitioned House	30
Village Fugitive	32
Green Time	33
Place Maritime	34
When the days are long in May	36

II

A Present from Sor Juana Inez de la Cruz	39
A Quechua Confession Manual (1584)	40
Scanno Abruzzo 1953	42
The Blessed Virgin appears to my friend Maureen	43
The Woman from McKenna & Co	44
The Uses of Disappointment	45
Jealousy	46
Envoy	48
Thermidor	50
The Art of War	51
Fisherman	52
Sha-tin Brides	53
Institute of Nuclear Medicine	54
Special Care Baby Unit	55
Midnight Gardeners of the Adonis Gardens	56
The Practice of Running	58
The Trespasses of Hens	60
Jack Lattin of Morristown	61
Hotel Placid	62
En Route	63
A Sleeping Spell	64

*to the late Julia Casterton,
poet and poetry teacher*

A Quechua Confession Manual

I

Aren't lovers always arriving at each other's boundaries?
— Rilke: 4th Duino Elegy

Internal Exile

Let's go tomorrow, live in a small town
with three bridges and a river running through,
where everyone's a stranger, we're not known.

A low-roofed house standing on its own,
no gates or hedge, a creaky glass lean-to.
Let's go tomorrow, live in a small town.

We'll walk the High Street on the note of noon,
visit dark parlours at the back of shops, go
where everyone's a stranger, we're not known.

Feed the stray dogs, slipping out at dawn;
at the plain butcher's, stay silent in the queue.
Let's go tomorrow, live in a small town

where a path slopes by a bean-field, down
to the river-bank, through a copse of red willow.
Where everyone's a stranger, we're not known.

When we leave who'll notice that we've gone?
We'll make no friendships, nothing to undo.
Let's go tomorrow, live in a small town
where everyone's a stranger, we're not known.

Pollux and Castor, elephants

Preparez -vous a des ragouts, / De rats aux champignons d'egouts.
—*Victor Hugo, Paris 1870*

Krupps' cannons pound the walls,
the darkness smells of soil and gas;
at Voison's, rue Cambon, a special black card
buys *sauce souris* on pate of rat.

It's a challenge to garnish donkey with cèpes;
there's a gold market for cats of all colours.
Castor feels itching deep in his trunk,
Pollux walks in the snow and shivers.

The gates of the Jardin des Plantes have been chained
for over a week, but now carts from de Boos
are waiting outside. Zebras are easy, Martin the bear
puts up a fight, now they draw on a ruse

and Adolphe Lebeeque, whom Castor knows well
wheels out the last kilos of branches and fruit
which he tips at the base of their sandpaper tree
as others take aim from the rainwater butt.

Grey lumps too big to be dragged,
so they're jointed there in a scratch abattoir.
Feet sliced away first, and eager talk spreads
to long lines outside the Boucherie Courtier.

A starving gourmet hurries out, to catch
the carrier pigeon's fragile message,
which unfurled, says, *Yes.* There's 'variety meat'
in a siege menu of elephant blood sausage.

Goncourt dines at seven, the evening sky
is brilliant with the enemy's flares.
There's *Consomm' Oliphant, filet de mulet*
and rarest, by Choron, the *Trompe Sauce Chasseur,*

nearly spoiled by Adolphe, who wept bitterly,
gripping dead Castor's trunk in the snow.
The butchers were waiting to finish their work:
C'est foutu Adolphe! But he wouldn't let go.

Hackney Blue Hour

What's left of day
between five and seven
is yellow sunlight
reflected on the Lea canal.

It lights up passages
between the warehouses,
the turrets of the hospital, your
long apartment window.

Tiger-marks your studded door,
your aluminium bell, catches
the black and white tiled floor
that winds through every room

with different meanings:
a *nurikabe* puzzle in the hall
rinsed purity in the bathroom
a salon rich and stern.

Bedroom Ware

Keeping a plate of black stones by the bed
imperfect pebbles, snowflake obsidian,
the marks, you said, like fingerprints.

I want to lick the lipstick off your teeth,
place my thumbs to iron out the creases
in your neck, follow with my palm
your back's uneven signature, ask
you to shake your hair down, let it hang
down for me, join the folded impressions
those like us have made in this space,
feel the outline of other people's limbs
from previous or future times.
Have all beds been slept in already?
I hope so or it means we'll have to undertake
a lot of work.

Thinking this in the unlit time before
an early morning white as starch
in the guard position by the door.

Dreaming of the Dead

This dark room is hung about with plaques
engraved with charities of the dead.
Wide, red-lipped faces in their frames stare back:
their painted eyes burn unforgivingly.
They'd rather be alive like us, instead.

The dead are tedious, each one of them ignores
the wisdom of Montaigne's remark
as has been done for you, make way for others.
But they're reluctant, like to sidle back
using your dreams for their amusement park.

Shameless, they yell, *remember me?* or want
to play Hitchcock, bobbing into frame
as plumbers, flower-sellers, 'man-in-lift',
small parts, to see if they extract your tears
or make you want to know them.

Sometimes they use complete disguise.
You wonder why you lose your strength
visiting a house you cannot recognise,
feel torn with sadness at the spectacle
of a white cat pawing uneven stairs.

They steer our dreams; they have to mourn
what used to be, dream of us, anticipate
which ones are soon to be arranged in uniforms.
Like them, we'll have to learn the graveyard skills:
how to contrive bold Purgatory hats.

Border Crossing

I must get down from the night train,
desert the dreaming coach, let the curtains remain
brushing heated windows, and set out on foot
printing the snow beneath my shiny boot.
This is the border and your country's edge.

Here, pine saplings are stripped new and white
like nerves. Come sunrise, they are trapped in light
falling on sidings, huts or a shivering gull's breast,
the guard's epaulettes; intensifying the orange zest
of barley sugar neon round the national badge.

In the small apartment block, dull lamps come on;
policemen's children argue and scoff breakfast. I'm here alone
with my identity papers curled inside my glove,
my clothes richer than myself. I hope to prove
why I'm seeking to stay. There's no hedge

to my bets — these red-stamped papers are made by me.
Any fine-line faults he detects, I'm arrested immediately.
He'll hunt me with heavy dogs as I break out across
already melting fields. Who cares? I'll run for it. They'll toss
my cards in the bin. At your city of lights beyond the ridge,

hitching tankers on the autobahn, ignoring the slush, I will arrive
filled with your territory. I'll be your scholar, hear your life,
hold your hand. We'll spoon dark meats, lie low, stare at the flood
rising up the bridge. Stand talking under trees. Share our reward
from tournaments, like joyous people of a golden age.

No, wait. What if it proves impossible for us?
Reflecting, you might just buzz
security, phone someone in authority
on a hotline. I'll be handed to the military.
What's done can be undone; our past can change.

Public Art

In the last century, polio charities placed statues of young victims which functioned as collecting boxes, in the public spaces of towns and cities.

Turn the tiled bend of Rufus
Street and anyone can see her
standing on the dry lawn of Hoxton Square.

Your eye is caught by a blue
out of place, not sky, but the blue
of her flaring dress. She's twenty feet high.

Up in the plane tree's netting,
her curls are custard yellow.
Nothing perches on her head, which is too startling

like the pipes of her legs
cased in brown iron braces,
crippled and cemented to her square begging base.

Peer between her legs
under the thick arch of her skirt
and see nothing but a wipe of smooth plaster.

The girl's hard hand holds out
a collecting box whose slit
is false; you couldn't donate to it even if you cared.

In the last century
there would have been real money.
Beheading, or breaking her box, common crimes.

Lucia's sky-blue cupboard

I'm going to put Lucia here
so when you're staring at her photograph

waiting for her image to register, peering
at the details of her dress, black taffeta,

with peonies sewn on by hand, the glow
of her shoulders under her shawl,

a high comb fixed like a window grille
in her polished hair, the mother-of-pearl

shoe-buckles, you'll realise that others
filling her with meanings is what she's thought about.

She stares at you with bright Euskara eyes
down a long nose, her broad throat

tattooed gold, an empress in disguise
knowing already how you'll speculate

on the silk waterfall of her underskirt,
crannies ribboned and ruched.

In her sky-blue cupboard she keeps a skin-shirt
finer than all this, and in her secret hooch

hang clothes wrapped in white tissue,
things embroidered and airy, orpiment duchesse.

Her pleasure at knowing they are better,
her pleasure at not showing them.

Because We Are, I Think

Not the end of the universe, South London,
end of the universe. From the north side
of the Thames I can still pinpoint you

with the fine needle of my own compass,
see you lying in the dusty garden,
flattening the uncut grass.

There's a newspaper covering your clever head
too much red wine instead of lunch—
you've been drinking with the flies.

Your guardian angel is asleep and you,
anaesthetised, can't feel the running ants
leave their trail-scent across your foot.

Souvenir du Dr Jamain, a full Bourbon
rose, the colour of venous blood,
has fewer buds than last year.

The onyx one, shaded like skin under the nail
pokes extra lances through the hedge.
Ground elder, rank at the base

attracts the feral lovers of the neighbourhood.
Fresh ground elder, deceptive, green.
How could you, oh how could you.

She revisits the Embankment

When she tried earlier, the traffic drowned her out,
head-lights distracted her, but now it's very late—
yellow and blue are the only colours left
as she wakes, cramped on a Portland bench.
She sniffs the Thames, and in the lemon light
pulls out some paper, folds a triangular hat
and puts it on her Dachshund.
Their dance is stately, she and the dog
bump twice against each other and she sings:
I looked over Jordan, what did I see?

A light glows from the training sloop *Chrysanthemum*,
her voice is echoing across oily mud, to gulls
motionless on the sand-bar; while the tide pulls away
from the viaduct, the paper hat spins in the shallows
heading east, downstream, to the Tower and All Hallows.

Violet, Doris, Hilda, Joyce

The Fire-fighters Memorial near St Paul's Cathedral in London lists the women who died on active service in the Second World War

The Heinkel dumped on the *Three Feathers*,
the *Bridget Arms* and the *Doncaster Tap*,
burnt out the *Lord Cornlillie*.

Smoke, water, fire and glass
corpses of drinkers folded en masse,
embracing willy-nilly.

Women's Auxiliary Fire Brigade,
ladder, chloroform, flashlight, spade
ignore the blood pooling stickily.

Shirley, Dorothy, Babs and Pearl
roped like climbers along the wall,
hose down the roaring gulley.

Sandbags to the Slaughtered Lamb!
Gas alert at the Tinkers Dam!
Blackout the Isles of Scilly!

Joyce was crushed at the Coffee Docks,
Judy burnt at the Paraffin Works.
We don't know what happened to Milly.

Retribution

I am seeking a second opinion
about this patient, for I
have examined him and can find nothing wrong.

Mr Jovanovic complains of insomnia
and sees the morning whiten many a time
after a night stretched out by the TV
watching Judge Judy.
He can't believe the whiteness of her collar
neat as a little girl's.

He wishes he'd known someone like her.
Her brusque justice, sentencing one
who's alienated the affections of his neighbour's
bichon frise, to paying the dog's dentist,
or granting a grandchild custody of the old drooler.
Or making some cheapskate pay up.

Sometimes the square screen arches: a wood.
Peering between birch boughs he sees Judge Judy
has iron teeth which glint unpleasantly.
She wishes to investigate the mounds and hollows
of a distant field. But while it's night she can't.

Then confessionals with Tricia: choruses of women
wreak retribution on pencil-moustached boys.
The lads love the attention; few sense the danger
they are in. In that they resemble most of us,
Jovanovic says.

Mr Jovanovic has attempted self-treatment
by anointing his eyelids with lead. He has
removed his pyjamas, spotted as snakeskin,
lies naked under a blanket of grey wool
aware of the holes in his body, which glow for the Judge
to light her way to him.

Buddleia Detectives

Watch your step there is something not quite right;
birds do not nest here. On half stem, half stick,
our purple heads weigh heavy as we sway
in the wind that blows over waste ground.

Watching, we nod approval at the payback
of old scores. We honey-reek at fly-tippers
hear screams, mark bruises, watch
the blue cheeks of a strangled man decay.

Our days are brickwork and our nights
are stone. Nodding with butterflies we observe
the walks of women. Moving in closer
we tap and peer against the dirty glass

windows of a nearby house, searching for
something with our purple telescopes,
then shake our heads, reveal the white
shock of our under-leaves to the wind.

Our old veins wrinkle, because
there are things for which we have no words.
Fretful, we return to the precinct-house
and report to the marquisate of waste.

London Light

If the night sky in February were clear
I'd see Orion and the bulls eye Aldeberan,
brilliant Gemini and crossing the span
of Pisces, Venus going to the dark hemisphere
beyond the sun. Lower than anyone could ever hear,
there are songs from when the world began,
black holes are humming a bass pavane,
56 octaves below middle C, wide, austere.
But London light is syrupy, too strong
to see or hear through, it exhausts the night
creates insomniacs, throws out a glare
across flowers, making short shadows along
balconies, grass yellow at midnight;
siphons the world away within its stare.

To die is different from what anyone supposed

after Whitman

The green glass offices are full of lawyers
most of them young, black suited girls
with honey-streaked hair, pink youths in
linen shirts, staring, yawning, worrying
over details of divorces and taxation.
Wondering where they'll go when
they declare, *that's it, I'm fucked,*
noting with happiness, *it's bloody late.*

Japanese waiters in black and gold
serve them noiselessly like attendant spirits,
each girl's head is inclined as if she's balancing
a chaplet of roses. Briefly, before dark,
the sky turns mauve; they linger; they inhale
the pleasure of London: to be here is
to be deserving of love, of money. Luckier.

Morning Duties by Sunlight

I see my neighbour
out early to work
on his shining tractor,
crossing, re-crossing
between the vines.
The machine is humming,
grunting and puffing out
a following cloud that shimmers
between blue and green:
the colour of Myloxychlor,
Triademenol, Malathion.

Emperor of the Kitchen Garden

While I was away,
My neighbour created a garden
    adjoining mine,
  deliberate and green.
Each day it seems he
    adds something, spikes of
white leeks or aubergines that
    hang as lamps,
some energetic scarlet beans.
He brought me a bucketful
    of green peppers, glossy
thick as cheeks.
The rest he takes to market
    where he stands,
check-capped, with other sunburnt men
by crates of stubby, shiny
    yellow courgettes:
Emperors amongst their gold.

Insulting Peacocks

When walking unsoberly in the hot garden
of Avignon's Palais des Papes,
and seeing a peacock, blue behind a bush

dragging his tail in the dust looking bored
(though he is not bored, peacocks are never bored
simply engaged in narcissistic introspection)

and realising this, you begin to
fracture his fantasy, first barring
his high stepping way then shouting harshly,

you're just a common peafowl.
You may continue to deride his tail and parentage
till a point comes, I swear, for I speak from experience,

when he shudders his little crown, and huffed as a dowager,
with a sound somewhere between a slap and a rustle,
lifts that iridescent, quivering sheaf,

shakes out and spreads his magnificent fan
emerald and indigo, as much as to say,
bow down, unworthy drunk. And you will.

Menus for a Requisitioned House

Just now, I polished the long banister:
by six it will be smeared with sweat
from soldiers heaving themselves upstairs,
to shoot at lacy plasterwork, optics, that
orange screen-print of electric chairs,
shredding the plasma, picking at frescoes,
hacking the gold clasps that keep the roof secure.
I'll be making coffee for the General
any hour she wants. Watching out
for the Adjutant in his silver-white wig.
Then afterwards I'll rinse long glasses,
swab the marks away, go down and
set the sticky-traps, that's the pattern of my day.
Since the house was requisitioned,
I have been working hard, wiping out doubts.
I'm under scrutiny, slander creeps along the terraces
something is happening, I'm not sure what is.
I have hidden what I can—five
titanium screens, ampoules of lignocaine,
green feather tea, the chromium antiques,
a twentieth century device for purifying rain.
Each bedroom has its military quota.
At night some young man, his head full
of the day's work, will remove his silk absorber,
stare at the zinc crucifix, the pious triptych on the nursery wall,
reflect how bodies are just a set of facts in order or disorder.
The otters feed where the stream runs fast, they eat greedily.
The far bank is a forest older than I know;
it reaches beyond the border, dark spruce, white fescue
waiting to be scythed apart when outriders
their lights full on, come roaring through.
I understand sacrifice as well as any Egyptian
whether it's to one god or all of them
on smoking altars, or, like here, in snow.

I write menus: *pickelfleisch,* roast hare, a pan-fried
tailess trout, blood sausages, eels from the lake
with pepper pot soup; then study the furrowed lawn,
listen for news on a wind-up radio
or wrapped in my barathea overcoat
inspect the outbuildings. I choose
the long way round. I won't go in the Factory.

Village Fugitive

When it was over, they counted casualties:
Clement and Jean, brothers, were shot in Marseilles.
Four others, sent to Mauthausen
were buried now, their youthful photographs
icons in the graveyard.

One man came back and within a year had killed,
but no-one told the police.
They had never come to that village during the war,
stayed smoking in their well-lit block-house, only going out
to check the loads on lorries.

So he left and lived in the woods, which higher up
turn to forest. Some thought he was close by, others said
he'd climbed to a chapel where eight hundred years ago
a Pope had once said Mass.
Though people said they'd seen him — some claimed he often came
to the village after dark, it was one of those things
talked of less and less, then not at all.

In the forest the hunter's trails are marked with a blue dot
splashed on the tree trunks, but there are
other paths where now the grass is barely bent
which lead to ravines or to stony outcrops
with a view of the whole valley. There are shelters
built like a honey comb, no-one knows how old.
When you can at last see into their blackness
after the intense sun, you cannot tell
whether someone has been there.
He would be eighty-four by now.

Green Time

This is April, this is green time:
                    it pushed aside the whiteness
on apple and cherry, with surprising force.
Even the cypress columns put out
                    new points in a less sober shade.
Pale green silk, a vine leaf unfurls
from a chrysalis, no hint of its sum
                    bright and blood red toughness.
Now I understand grey almond green,
and the yellowish new oaks,
silver green aspens bright as sixpences.
                    All this on the ridge.

We who live this year have passed
                    death's gateway and come out the other side
leaving behind dark purples. *Reqonquista.*

There are small green grains on rye and wheat
and mauve and mint on lilac like a children's new sweetmeat.
                    The ivy puts out young and veinless leaves
all this on the ridge, the valleys and walls—
                    and on the mountain
                                        some shoots
patches of brilliance before the forest turns in on itself
     and its forms cannot be understood,

like the coming seriousness of fields

when the sun shines in the terrible months.

Place Maritime

The octopus lives,
a suburbanite;
builds a bailey of rocks
with balls on his gateposts
all twirled into place.
Water ghost of the Med,
hunted at night
by people whose ancestors
traced on their vessels,
his wide eyes, tough beak,
endless, spiralling arms.
His ink sac tugged off,
and his mantle of nerves—
a seaside cement mixer
softens him up. His coils
are removed, the glistening body
is cut up and stewed
until the rind glitters.
Whole babies like stars,
and a green chiffonnade.
As I'm spooning the daube,
smoke curls from the table
where Julie, *notaire,* smiles
at Mathilde, *dentiste,*
and wriggles her toes
inside her suede boots
thinking Mathilde
is morbid but handsome,
and doesn't say what's
on the tip of her tongue
but swallows a tentacle
soft disc and all.

And I think, oh Julie
what are we doing
slicing this sign
from the watery future?
We should rather decant
Greek fire down our throats.

When the days are long in May

Lanquan li jorn son lonc en mai
                                          —Jaufre Rudel

That evening you were vivid as the sign at Crazy Horse.
Winter suited you, making you darker,
not the pale man I had always thought—

your white cuffs shone under the lectern lights,
as you talked about *amor de lonh,*
unrolling speech like a carpet from Andalus.

No-one left early and I came out, a shade
among departing darker crowds.

April, we were called by friends
to a red American diner
where everyone looked cyanosed or worse.
They never showed; you asked,
do you think they'll make it?
as we stood up to go. You put your hand
on my shoulder and looked concerned.

It happened then. As at Easter when the sun tilts
flooding the simple gardens and filling their borders
with yellows, it seemed we tore through something
and came out gasping and streaked.
Blood moved under the blue fontanelles
of our new-born heads.

In May, we breathed as twins, plaited
like the high ridges of the Cordillera.

II

There are three trespasses of hens: swallowing bees, injury to the dye plants, and attacks on the garlic. A guilty hen shall have her feet tied together or rag boots put on.
  —Traditional Irish [Brehon] Laws, 1st century AD.

A Present from Sor Juana Inez de la Cruz

My dearest Marquesa —
what a silly quarrel
between two stargazers
about the rings of Saturn.

Where my telescope's concerned
I'm a possessive rogue:
It's about time I learned
your love is more important.

I'm going to make for you
posh as a Mayan prince
a sumptuous chocolate shoe
with sugar roses.

Chocolate calms fret and fever,
aids the digestion.
The Chocolate God of April
will solve the question.

High fashion shoe
with a long tongue.
Wear it or eat it —
dear friend, it's up to you.

Let us see eye to eye —
laugh again at the cerise
silk stockings of that young hidalgo
and his amazing codpiece.

A Quechua Confession Manual (1584)

Remember, in this hemisphere the stars
are different. Look up and see the Pleiades.
My brother, understand, the sins are different too,
that's why you'll need this book.
These people have no knowledge of concupiscence,
their only prohibitions are of rank
yet in their ignorance, immortal souls
are heading for Hell. It's not true by the way
that they have said they do not wish for heaven
if the Spanish are there.

This volume in their language will embrace
all possible offences of the flesh.
Learn it and rehearse your questioning
before you hold Confession.
Establish frequency, clarify with whom he sinned,
inquire if she's a virgin or the wife
of some *cacique*. For female penitents,
ask if they seduced a priest, or climbed
on top of a man, made love-philtres,
allowed unnatural practices.
Do not omit the question about llamas.

They should respect us more, but fifty years ago
even their slaves were dressed in gold
and thought they were the Children of the Sun.
Brother Felipe likes to tell the novices
of when he gave the Sacrament in Cuzco
the Inca prince and all his sons wore silver suits
and emeralds in bunches, big as the grapes
below Valladolid. Sometimes I think
they understand ecstasy — that day their bone flutes
played homage to the spilling of Christ's blood.

A quarter of a century has passed since
I've been home. I won't be going back
unless as Incas say, the sun should change.
Here's some advice for your first tour of duty:
before going out on pastoral visits
across these mountains and the highest snows
select the plumpest brother here as your companion.
He will sustain you with his dreams of food,
amuse you with a stock of impure stories. When
the puma that's been stalking you for days
leaps out in ambush you'll be sure that he
won't emulate your turn of speed.

Scanno Abruzzo 1953

At a faded corner of the street
they encounter each other: two
sixty year olds. He's walked up,
dusty from the dry red fields.
He looks at her neat boots,
the beading on her widow's hat,
hears her stiff dress rustle in the wind
and catches the glow of a pearl rosary
against her velvet collar.

He should have married her
when Alessandro fell off that roof.
As he stays muffled in the layers of his cape
she leans towards him, whispering about
her son and daughter in the city:
oh, the car factory, the gleaming cars
women's red nails, their white stiletto shoes
cucina blanca, Juve stadium,
huge buildings made of glass,
the via Roma shining like a mirror;
her son's *frigorifero*, whose hum kept her awake.

He thinks that she's become a bore
praising the city she's seen only once,
the children that have left and won't come back.
He doesn't nod agreement;
a morning shadow falls across the street
and tail lights moving down the hill
reflect in the *farmacia* door.
A sharp wind nags his skin;
he feels there's thunder somewhere North,
rain without purpose in the city, squalls
exploding on pavements, spattering the cars,
to disappear in drains, a waste, a waste of water.

The Blessed Virgin appears to my friend Maureen

Monday, mid-August, just before tea,
with waste-ground shadows on the grass,
we'd just finished saying the rosary.

Maureen whispered to me in a special low voice,
Our Lady is standing on that yellow bush—
I tried, screwed up my eyes to view

and thought I glimpsed a sky-blue sash,
a slim brown foot in a fine brown shoe.
It seemed quite normal that she'd appear

to two small girls in homemade cardigans,
but I wondered why she'd come to Lancashire.
Was it the coal shortage or to open a co-op,

see off the rich rude Protestants who ran
the only corner shop? Maureen was praying,
we might be Saints—I didn't like to say

we've got no lambs, we're near the road,
this isn't Portugal, anyway. But she
was dreaming of a Papal kiss, a canopy

of cloth of gold, conclaves of Cardinals.
I saw a snail crawl up the wall, the sticky
mud of cycle tracks, a pile of Guinness bottles,

our bright sweet-papers scudding wild.
She's fading slightly, Maureen said,
what sandwiches has your Mum made?

She grabbed the lemon curd and strawberry
and while she gorged, I pondered. I was not
a Chosen One. Do visions make you hungry?

The Woman from McKenna & Co

When you see the grey half-dozen
undertaker's men march up the aisle
flat-footed with a careful tread,
and they and the coffin almost comprising
a creature of brass and flesh, a flowery
duodecapod of wood and lead,
remember that in a quarter of an hour
they'll be lounging behind a pillar—
talking of shift duties. There's one who's short,
one with a greasy pompadour,
two who resemble the cadaver
and two with eyes of inappropriate blue
blowing clouds of heartless smoke
beside the crematorium flue.

But not the woman from McKenna & Co.
Tall, tightly belted, in her black coat
of office and buttoned leather gloves,
she began her funeral walk before Michael's hearse.
Behind her, all the cars revved up,
as the threatened rain from Ireland burst.
It trickled the grooves of her red plait
and soaked her to the bone.
Yet she strode the camber,
through rivers curling down the iron drain.
She didn't pause, completed her slow procession
past the damp gardens, down the plain road,
as if she, water-soldier, was keeping an oath
to march through Acheron.

The Uses of Disappointment

When it doesn't happen,
that is sometimes as comfortable
as Aunt Jago's cashmere cardigan
whose violet-grey has never shown the dirt.

You don't have to consider
barbaric gilding on a turquoise egg,
the likely destruction of a red
or yellow form inside.

The canopies of trees remain
as better shelter than the pink
silk of a ceremonial howdah
rubbing grooves in the elephant's back.

The oesophagus stays clear and
ears are open to cathedral sounds,
your saliva keeps as sweet as you
might ever muskily allow.

Admire the beige outlook.
Fine grained corners of an empty box,
the mercurial dissolution of sharp,
the rubbery sensation at the edge of perish.

Jealousy

I can go blind with watching or lose
the connection of brain and eye

so even inanimate things start to move round
in complicated ways, make sounds like

bellows or punctured bladders thrown from a height.
The smallest things matter. There is a black

white-headed bug in my house and whether he's
skating the slats of the Venetian blind falling

into the red folds of the carpet or just sauntering
across the bathroom tiles he knows more than I.

My fingers separate the blind so I can peer
at the hard glare of the world.

The bug sees sunlight striped across my face,
turning me zebra. The bug rolls up into

a mottled bead, he's specially coated thin and flexible,
bloodless with soft parts and so I flick him on the floor.

Someone who's cut the letter Y in me
from belly to neck is opening up the flaps to take a look.

But when it's over and the membranes are stretched out
and dried, each organ has been weighed and

residues are rinsed away, I feel a stateliness.
Then I can say: go out under a big sky,

look as far as you can. Perhaps the sun will
vapourise the aromatic oils of your head,

bleach your yellow hair. And I can stop
digging out my shadow.

Envoy

They find him a quarter
in the thousand year old Termitary
and welcome him to a place
bluer than earth, with holartic
lakes of sombre yellow,
forests of cities, called Gibraltar
Urumqi, Calgary, which glow
like lava, a hundred *versts* below.

At first, they like him
but for all the wrong reasons—
a ponderous official hat, tall chitin shoes.
Everyone is chlorotic, their blood
has too much salt, they love disputes—
think his imported methods close to mutiny;
language misers, with one word for all grades
of humiliation and a type of lamprey.

He was warned before he left:
they hate to be divided by taste;
each new envoy's ugliness
generates cruel comment, even outrage,
then green flows across, he sheds nakedness,
becomes part of the landscape. An experiment,
makes no contribution to knowledge
without before and after measurement.

Despite the exhausting darkness
of the Termitary, he finds it's tomorrow
every ten hours. Autumn and spring
are the only two seasons, joined red at the edge.
What keeps him is their skill at building
air gardens, the regattas and races, his own
addiction to sympathy, perfect whiteness and sortilege.

The ticking red and blue light
of the departure craft landing in an ice storm
brings on full anamnesis of the years
spent in the Planetary Library, the exact form
of the vaults where they keep their effigies.
He's stopped the law suits against flying insects
and bringing animals to trial and death.
No-one is seeking his replacement.

Thermidor

From the wetlands outside the walls
the stalking white cranes who pick grubs
from their home in the grass mat, fly away,
and sphagnum turns lime green, and soaked.
Our city takes to the water, a galleon.
It is not as if we don't know, in fact
we watch fascinated, fixed like one
who can tense nothing but his eyelash.
At midday, light is thick although
the orange lights provide some penetration.
We are waiting for evening, then night.

A wet mist has hung around for months,
like an enormous moth, sometimes ice-chips
have filled up the fire exits, to be shovelled
in handfuls until we are frost burned.
There's no plan, just watching, as reddish water
fills the streets and noises become buried,
the archives are flooded and down there
the only sounds are the last words of lifts,
queuing systems and automatic gates.

We've seen saints in the streets, yelling
about what could be saved, walking ankle deep
eyes boiling with need, in the sandy piazzas,
by office towers and dark markets. One
has hefted a load of cedar wood in the hope
of getting out, he's looking for living ballast.
The task, though, is to get rid of stuff, all the wiring
that we hold so dear and when
it's completely hooded, thrown out over the walls,
we'll imagine our futures, the small way we'll live
after the rain gates have been locked.

The Art of War

Look upon your soldiers as beloved children and they will willingly die with you.
— *General Sun Tzu*

The young man unties
the white silk scarf
from around his head.

Unclips his arrows,
lays them at his mother's feet,
shows her his wound.

My general anointed my
flesh himself and fed
me daily from a spoon.

On hearing this,
she begins to wail
and tear her blue apron.

Fisherman

I watch him set up by the Danger notice
on the Song dynasty bridge.
Bamboo rod arced, he braces rubber sandals
against the concrete bank and casts in the canal.
Soon there's a bite, a splash, a big grouper
with nickel body and Imperial yellow head
is swung onto the cement where the fisherman
unhooks him, cuts the gills and drops the fish into
the plastic bag from Five Red supermarket,
dangling from his Flying Pigeon bike.
Ignoring me, silent European
he rummages more bait and casts again.
After a minute, from the bag, a rustle, then a flap,
a louder rustle, a tearing sound, a beat, a batter,
the bag convulses, jumps, the grouper undulates
with primal electricity that's patterned there from tail to head.
The old bike shudders on its rusty foreleg.
It takes as long as twenty minutes, then,
occasional whispers in the plastic folds become
small movements, gentle twitches.
How lazy the big-eared gods of fish.
The man, meanwhile, stays hunched and once again
lowers his rod into the black water.
Dredgers are scooping sea bed and floor,
grating canal, mixing coast and creek.
The isthmus will sprout all-night factories,
glow-worms across the delta of the Pearl.
Each day, dust screens the sun that should be there.
I sprint home panting in the leaden air.

Shatin Brides

Shatin, New Territories, China

First week of the Ox Year
is the busiest of the lot:
bride after bride will stand here
before the lens, impermeable to weather
rubbing the public grass out
greening her white slipper.

Freshly escaped from the ceremony
a flock of conjuror's doves
are smiling and pouting, in puffy
perfect whiteness of hired gowns:
one smoothes her satin gloves
her jet eyebrows shine like calligraphy.

After the photos, brides go back to factories
assembling electric parts, machining clothes.
Change into a red dress for evening revelries.
Just now, they'll take a moment to surmise,
chilled as the spring wind blows:
Into whose courtyard has my flower fallen? Why?

Institute of Nuclear Medicine

The very small is why this place exists,
a site for looking at infinity.
Here, one needs the hearing of an ant.

Attuned outside the normal frequency there is
awareness of the hiss of lemon lights,
the sound a hand makes when it moves,

slip of a needle as it probes a vein,
clack of a syringe, and whisper of filling blood.
A paper gown crackles from its casing,

a paper cup has oilier sound,
a lower crunching note.
No chance to hear the noise of waves

bouncing back from denser tissue,
nor sounds of liquid flow between
four chambers of the heart

but the gamma camera clicks as metal plates
the colour of an ice-cream maker
transmit in greyscale places never seen,

with intimacy closer than a lover.
Blood circles the ear like the sighing
remembered in a seashell's whorls and

courses through labyrinths.
Stuck to the moulded couch,
a body strains and creaks,

as rigging on some ancient yacht
bent in a strong gale before returning
shore-wards to the estuary.

Special Care Baby Unit

Blue-green light
in the bubble
turns your skin

a raw hue,
your day-old
shiny skin.

Ventilator, plastic,
white and serious.
A grown-up thing.

Your fragile chest,
a nipple like a pink
seed pearl.

Soft little shorts,
boxing gloves of gauze,
my sporting girl,

in your bubble,
clasp my finger
in your fist.

Midnight Gardeners of the Adonis Gardens

All afternoon they've lain in bed
watching the slow unfurling of white curtains

or sitting up to see the one ship in the bay
cutting like a knife through silk,

as the sun swallows all the shadows,
and blots each pool of black.

Only the Dog Star grows in August.
Hidden in daytime, he roars out at night

to add to the seasonal cacophony
of an outbreak of female carrying on.

Almost midnight and skirts bunched,
they're up the ladders to the roof.

Women from all over town, whatever
their age or reputation, are hauling

rough pots of red and black, each with
a fuzz of growth, sprouting new green.

They whirl torches, strike drums
bound with tin, carry jugs running over

with wine and water, quantities of wet,
and don't care if they spill them as they climb.

Once up, they dance and celebrate all night
keeping the town awake with their singing,

so loud even the fish in the bay can hear.
They rouge each other's breasts, shout out indecencies

and turning on their little potted gardens say,
We've planted you and now we're leaving you

your shoots will shrivel and turn brown
you know without our care you can't survive.

The curly lettuce shiver in their urns, expelled
from those sheltering arms. Gently the women spread

the pots out on their sides as Aphrodite
laid Adonis when she'd done with him.

The Practice of Running

Described by Sidney G. Osborne
in Gleanings from the West of Ireland *1847*

We took the best grey
when we set out that morning
to know the state of the country
between Leenane and Westport.

Not a beast, flying insect or bird,
everywhere just an absence,
yet a white new road, narrow
ending halfway up a hill.

Down she came running,
about twelve years old, barefoot
a man's old jacket buttoned to the neck.
She fell in beside us, going fast

and did not look at us nor hold
out a hand but ran deliberately
at the speed of the grey, though
we told her over and over

that we'd offer her nothing.
She kept a pace matching ours
and at each quarter mile,
my friend shook his head,

though fascinated by the way
her naked legs, like spokes, seemed
to draw power from the turning wheels.
A few times I saw him weaken, I

told him no, angry at her persistence,
while over the holes and stones
she sped her way unfaltering,
her eyes on the road, her feet

a light slap above the noise of wheels
and creaking seats. Two miles
and more she ran, and then
looked hot and gave a cough,

and with a leap, increased her speed
which broke my friend at last:
he steadied himself, half rose
and threw her four-pence.

The Trespasses of Hens

Tall white hen of the bright eye
and scarlet jester's cap you've strayed
from the apple orchard to the plots nearby.

You squeezed through a slit on the dark
side of the withy fence into the sunlight,
snowy feathers sheening like the bark

of silver birch after a Samhain frost.
You knocked upon the hives and in your soft
swallowing of bees a season's grubs were lost.

Next, to my dye plants, burdock and beet
bedstraw and woodruff, my flax and sorrel
all trampled by your cinquefoil ivory feet.

Red berries too high for you, my polished haws
but you scratched up wild garlic and a late
crop of sweet roots with those trowelling claws.

To all of us the Brehon law applies:
so for my own and for my neighbour's sake
your coral legs I'll bind with gentle ties
cut from the linen of my earth-stained skirt.

Jack Lattin of Morristown

A wager dreamt up on a noisy evening
with him back from Paris talking in French
in a Kildare accent, calling for oysters,
the candlelight there making everything mauve
but the jet on his waistcoat and round wigless head
black-fuzzed, his huge eyes as bright as a frog's.
Cloncurry was there, Rahilly the poet
Lady Mary's daughters, Begnet and Clare
their hair twined about with organza ribbons,
not blue as expected but indecent yellow.
And all of us laughing as he made the bet
uncrossing silk legs on the tapestry cushion,
bowing towards the ornate velvet chair
then leaping impatiently on to the table,
the rush of his movement extinguished the candles:
the devil is in me to dance twenty miles,
from this house to Dublin, new steps every furlong,
Larry Grogan come with me, I'll fiddle, you'll pipe!

His faced glowed as red as coals in the grate
while I started a reel to get him in practice
and he danced out the door, it was two in the morning
with a summer moon over the silver white road,
and he danced and caught up those going to market
who cheered him, bent down under firkins of butter.
Past hawthorn, past barley, past old Castle Mansfield,
he wore out the patents, insulted the leather
the whistling and cheering frightened the thrushes,
crows flapped away senseless, the liveries alarmed,
no rest at crossroads, no stopping at ditches,
drinks on the move to the gates of the city
and Rahilly, Wogan and Walsh there to greet him.
The work of his heart was more than his years—
this fiddler, this dancer was danced black and blue
he died the next day, not quite twenty-two.
Oro! Oro!, brave Jacky Lattin.

Hotel Placid

Outside the gates people are washing, making breakfast or fires.
Someone will lay out on the pavement a set of oracle bones,
an arrangement of all parts of a bicycle.

He is conscious of the maid in short white socks
nudging a squeaking trolley over tiles,
as she ferries the stained sheets, comes back with the clean.

The russet water from his tap smells sulphurous,
contains, he thinks, medicinal properties;
weekly moppings twirl dust devils into corners

where they lie waiting, curled and soft.
A grey carpet conceals more skin cells than the bed.
On an abacus of gristle he calculates how many.

Once, his window was left open accidentally;
something got in, thudding like a sack of meal
on the dark furniture, no sound came from its mouth.

He realised when it had gone, leaving a splintered frame
the tiling soiled, that all the space above him
and below, seemed bigger than before.

They said the visit meant misfortune;
but he had always believed in the shiftingness of things—
felt lucky to have been the focus of its orange eye.

En Route

Renew the manicure kit, polish my nails,
buy some gold lacquer for use there.
I'll dye my braids red and shine my skin.
I know how to massage hands, to oil them,
how to wrap fingers in wax.

The stop and start of the train, going through palm trees
leads to the other side of the sugar river where we unload.
A battered old flat-back bounces us to the airport.
The guards wear green uniforms, carry bright guns
and scare us with their laughs.

But they're not going anywhere, they can only stand and sweat.

At the cool end of the day when the orange sun dissolves
we take off, crammed in the airbus bound
for Brazzaville. My brother cries, he's thirsty,
but there's nothing for us until we meet my uncle in the city.

We're going to Europe.
In my mind I see concrete barriers, cafes, new cars, rain,
dogs with little coats, loved by their blonde owners.
I practice my speech to the women of Paris,
using nothing the nuns have taught:
Mesdames, voici la plus belle methode africaine.

Below, the forest has no lights.

A Sleeping Spell

I draw a circle round this space—
Lie here and let your longings fall
Lie in the green

The circle spins a flawless dream:
Friends you have lost are all restored
Lie in the green

The circle folds its sweet curve round
You'll rest on seas as warm as milk
Lie in the white

From the green forest breathe in deep
Its floor contains no trace of harm
Lie in the green

Settle the darkness at the edge—
Three beeswax candles' yellow light
Honey the air

Pavilion safer than the womb,
A gentleness of hand and eye:
Lie in those arms

Here all the colours of the earth
Are painted on a richer shore—
The world's more perfect than a sphere

Sleep in the green